How to ⟍   *thrives in the midst of crises*

.the importance of family

By Willie Reid

The Importance of Family - How to ensure your family thrives in the midst of crises

Copyright © 2007 by Willie Reid
reid62@msn.com

p. cm.
ISBN: 978-0-9658629-6-7
Printed in the United States of America

1. Reid, Willie   1st Printing 2008

Table Contents

ACKNOWLEDGEMENTS

I want to thank my wife Gloria Hollingshed Reid and my dear children Lorea, Willie Jr. (affectionately known as El) and Ryan. Without them I would not be the man I have become today nor would my ministerial mission have been as successful as it has been. For their support in being a part of this book, I also want to thank my sisters Virginia and Carolyn, and my brothers Hildred (deceased), J.W., Robert David, Howard and Frederick. To Fellowship Bible Baptist Church, my second home and my second family, thank you for your support and love over the past 27 years.

Additional thanks go out to my pastor friends and brothers in Christ, specifically my nephew Pastor Donald Reid of Alethia Baptist Church, Macon, GA; Pastor E. Dewey Smith, Jr. of Greater Travelers Rest Baptist Church, Atlanta, GA; and Pastor Craig Oliver of Elizabeth Baptist Church, Atlanta, GA. I must also thank my spiritual mentors over the years: my father Pastor J. W. Reid, Sr. (deceased), Pastor Harold Rawls (deceased), Pastor Walter Glover, Pastor Jasper Williams and Pastor Rick Warren.

ABOUT THE AUTHOR

Pastor Willie L. Reid, Sr. grew up a pastor's son in Eatonton, GA. After working several years in the sales industry, he received the call to start a new church in Warner Robins, GA in 1980. Starting with a storefront property and just two people, Pastor Reid shepherded Fellowship Bible Baptist Church into the 3,000 member congregation it is today. He speaks extensively on the subjects of family and pastoral life. Pastor Reid and his wife Gloria, the proud parents of three grown children, live in Kathleen, GA.

INTRODUCTION

Family. Family has been the motivating force in my life for over 30 years, and will continue to be such until my death. Family is what drives people to succeed, and is grounded in the earliest stories and most sacred unions of the Bible. One of the greatest honors bestowed upon a man is God's call to lead a family, and I have been fortunate enough to lead two – my home and my church. My home family has shaped me and driven me as I've led my other family – Fellowship Bible Baptist Church. The two have grown together, faced trials together, and have become so intertwined that they could be considered one, but are separate units that enjoy different aspects of a father's love and care. My two families have helped one another and sharpened one another, giving true meaning to the concept of a village raising a child. We have been a bound community, reliant on one another for survival and for support in an every developing relationship with God. Both of my families have taught and challenged me, but most importantly, they have required me to rely on the Lord's guidance in everything I do. After all, God is our supreme example of a family leader. He leads us, the entire world, as His children. He created each of us to face triumphs and challenges, all for the purpose of helping us live out our life's purpose – to honor and glorify Him. If I've learned one thing in building and leading my home and church families, it is that without God, neither will function nor prosper to its full potential.

My first family officially formed on June 8, 1973 when Gloria and I became husband and wife in the living room of my parent's home. We first met when I worked at Sears and Roebuck in Warner Robins. I greeted her, but she didn't hear me, so I thought she was just ignoring me because she wasn't interested in talking with me. A short time afterward, a mutual friend introduced us. When I explained to her that she was the girl who ignored me, she claimed to have never heard me. Gloria is the kind of woman who guards herself well and makes sure she knows you before she lets you into her mind and her life. Needless to say, she did her research on me before she would agree to go out on a date. Somehow I wrapped her up and after nine months of dating and engagement, we were married.

Unfortunately, this family started under the guise of a Godly relationship, lacking the true faith and discipline required to honor the Lord. I was convinced I was a Christian, and decided that meant I could do whatever I wanted; I was saved after all. Having grown up a pastor's child, I considered my salvation secure in my heritage, and in doing so, preferred to live my life as I saw fit. It was the fast life for me, but one teeming with insecurity and jealousy.

Gloria suffered some because of my attitude, facing my jealousy and enduring my need to dictate and rule, rather than love and lead. But God had other plans in store for my family and me. Despite my ignorance and pride, our faithful Lord brought me to an understanding of the true meaning of salvation and wiped the scales from my eyes. I was set free to start anew. Afterward, every day took on a new meaning as I was transformed into a new man and we became a new family.

With a fresh perspective and the truth of God's Word in my life, I began to change and to shape my family in a new way. Suddenly, serving Gloria became my purpose as the leader of our family. I loved God and Gloria and put them before myself, something I'd never experienced before. We sought the Lord together and built one another up in love. My family was feeling something it had never felt before – the love of God and the joy of salvation.

Several years after I committed my life, God called me to start another family, a different family. Gloria and I had been attending a local church and were happily and faithfully involved as leaders and teachers. We were soon approached with the prospect of planting a church, and with the help of the Lord, proceeded to do so. My second family began just as the first family had – humbly, but this time without any pretense. We were held together by God, who filled us with His love, so much so that little room was left for great doubt. Through our early struggles, the Lord was faithful as always, helping me lead and giving me a heart to save the lost at any cost. With that, Fellowship Bible Baptist Church was born.

Despite having grown up in a minister's family, I was not always aware of a pastor's priorities. As is the case with so many pastors, church directors, missionaries, and even lay people, I felt my father placed priority on the church more often than his family. This experience and my own experiences as a pastor taught me that a pastor's priorities start with God, continue to his family and finally arrive with his church. It may have taken me a while to reach that revelation, but I eventually discovered that this order is the only acceptable way for a leader to be effective. For that matter, it is the order every Christian should follow. I don't claim to have ever gotten it perfectly right, but through a concerted effort I quickly learned that order is a requirement for a pastor to be relevant to the congregants at church and his family at home. In the end, that order and that life come down to faith and family.

I've been a story teller most of my life. I'd love nothing more than to sit down with you and tell you how God has changed my life and given me two families to lead. For now this book will have to suffice. Throughout my life a myriad of people, places and events have influenced me. The greatest of these have been the Lord and my two families. They have molded me into the man I am today. Sermons. Weddings. Funerals. Football games. Track meets. Cookouts. Festivals. Bible studies. Family dinners. My life has been filled with more memories than I can express, but the ones that seem most relevant, most important in my growth as a Christian man and a human being, are included here. I haven't founded a today. But today is different than any other day. I've spent years as a salesman; they say I'm natural-born. I'm not selling anything today though. We spent two weeks searching out a place to meet and finally found a one room vacancy at Building 10 in Buzzell Village on Watson Boulevard in Warner Robins, GA. My new family's new home. Gloria and I don't know what will happen today. I don't know what I've gotten myself into. I'm at the point of lacking any expectation other than the Lord will be faithful to us. We might have a Bible study between the two of us, but we're hoping for more. I look myself in the mirror and see the sleep draining from my eyes as the Spirit of the Lord fills my heart with joy. I think we are going to be alright. Save the lost at any cost – that's my mission. Off to work.

A new church hasn't been started or built in Warner Robins in many years. There is so much to do and think about in trying to start one, and I don't have many people to look to because we are about to do a new thing. Now I'm trying to start the second full-time, every-Sunday black church in Warner Rob-

1

THE FIRST DAY

It's early. The sleep in my eyes makes my vision blurry. Do I really need to wake up already? I roll out of bed and sit, thinking about waking up and collecting enough thoughts to make my feet take me to the bathroom. Step one. Step two. My momentum takes me the rest of the way to the bathroom. The cold water feels good and alerts my senses to the fact I am awake. Then it hits me. I am Willie Reid and today is the first day of existence for Fellowship Bible Baptist Church.

It's February 10, 1980 and I have to go to work

Fortune 500 company or become president of a country. I don't have a multi-platinum album and I have yet to win a Nobel Prize. I am simply a man with two families. And this is the story of how they grew.

ins. How did I get here? Several years ago I was living and working in Macon, GA, having just dropped out of college. My sister Virginia asked me to move down here with her and her son. I was called to preach the gospel in 1978, and here I am.

Matthew 28:19-20. That scripture has been engrained in my mind for weeks. "Go ye therefore, and teach all nations, baptizing them in the name of the Father, and of the Son, and of the Holy Ghost; teaching them to observe all things whatsoever I have commanded you: and, lo, I am with you always, even unto the end of the world. Amen." I would get up in the middle of the night and think about Matthew 28:19-20. And so I finally surrendered myself to it.

Gloria has been with me all the way. I'm fortunate to have someone who supports me like she does, more importantly someone who supports God's call like this. I remember when we first became true Christ-followers and started reading the Good News Bible every day. With each sitting we would understand more about God and learn more about His people and His will.

It seems like just yesterday I was being asked to lead a Sunday school class at The Greater Springfield Bible Baptist Church. It was so daunting that I initially refused. I didn't think I was ready for that job and sometimes I wonder if I'm ready for this one. Of course, I relented back then because no one else would do it. There has been a little more thought and preparation going into the move of starting a church. I hope those who come think I'm fun since I've always tried to teach in a fun way. At the very least, the teenagers always liked me. Enough postponing, I've got to get to the church.

So here I am. We haven't heard of any adults who plan to come today, but anyone would be nice. Whenever two or more are gathered together in God's name, He is surely there with them. As I arrive, I'm thinking Gloria had better make sure she gets here. No use in talking to myself.

I spent all last night trying to meditate on my notes, prepare for my first big sermon. I prayed, studied, reviewed and prayed some more. It's wise to study and review scripture passages over and over again because there is always something else to learn. The hardest thing to do as a pastor is getting through to your congregations. People always say they understand what you're saying, but most of the time they really don't get it. They aren't taking it in. The only thing you can do, though, is keep teaching and trust God is going to open their hearts, ears and minds so they can truly understand.

What's interesting to me is that I want plenty of sinners in here today and in the days after that. Christ can work in the heart of a sinner and I can teach, mold and help a sinner. Christians who are interested in going to church but don't want to learn and be taught to win souls to Christ are wasting their own time. They make me frustrated for the most part, but I guess they need to hear the Gospel as much as the lost. I hope they will come as well. It's comforting knowing God can do anything in the heart of anyone at anytime, otherwise I might end up being some sort of colossal failure. Enough talk about failing. This is supposed to be a victory. The first day of church. I'm scared. I'm excited.

2

THE TWO FAMILIES

After that first service I knew the Lord was going to hold us in His hand. Of course, doubts can creep into everyone's mind. Sometimes they can be harmful, but when used correctly, doubts can strengthen our faith. I'd go so far as to say they can be helpful in that they force us to seek out the truth. Fortunately, the truth is in God, and I'm always led back to Him through the toughest questioning times.

There is no higher calling than a local pastor. Many people think that the president of the United States of America holds the most important position in the world, but it's actually the local pastor. Any person can become the president, but not anyone can be a pastor. A pastor has to hear from God and shepherd a congregation. I've always scoffed at the idea of becoming the president – I would have to give up a higher calling.

Starting a church and starting a family are similar events. They generally begin with a minimal amount of people with a minimal amount of knowledge and a maximum amount of faith. Both involve fears and risks, but both lead to incredible fulfillment and immense joy. Gloria was always with me 100 percent. As we worked together to grow the church, she taught the children and I taught the adults. Every Saturday we went out to witness in the neighborhood, going door-to-door and focusing ourselves on preaching Christ to our community. Some people would accept Christ and come to our church, some would accept Christ and go to another church, and sometimes it was hard to see potential members go somewhere else. But we remembered that it was more crucial that these people be saved and know Christ than it was for them to come to our church. So we continued going out to minister and reach out to others.

The most important constant in starting a family and a church is faith in Jesus Christ. With Christ, all things are possible according to God's will. With Christ, we are free if we will allow ourselves to be. We need only trust in God's promise.

Gloria and I continued to pour ourselves into Fellowship. I wouldn't let anyone from our home church join our new church because I wanted people to know that we were serious about this new work. We were looking to build a movement in Warner Robins, not just have people transfer memberships so we could feel good about ourselves. While we received support from others, Gloria and I took the majority of the load on our own shoulders. That is how I know God was with us through those early years because we couldn't have done it on our own. He took us from that first building in Buzzell Village into a larger one in the same complex in just six months. Gloria, a public school teacher, was able to bring children from her classes to church. For a while our church generally consisted of Gloria, myself and as many children as we could fit into our van. When you reach children, you reach parents as well, and with that in mind, we continued to meet with the children. Sure enough, the kids enjoyed church enough that their parents began coming and getting involved. Our family was growing.

At home our family was growing as well. Gloria and I had tried to have children in the past, but a series of pregnancies had ended in miscarriages and stillbirths. We were both devastated, but we had faith that the Lord would bring us children if it was in His will. After all, Abraham and Sarah waited until she was 90 years old to bear children. We knew God would bring us children in His timing, not ours. Faith-fulness was the only option.

Then, a year after the birth of our church, God blessed us with the birth of our daughter Lorea. Re-lief. As I stared down at that beautiful baby girl, I couldn't help but be amazed at the wonder of God's creation. I now had two burgeoning families, two families to lead and two families to grow. God was paralleling the growth of our family with the growth of our church, slowly bringing me along to make sure I was up to the challenge of leading His children.

God calls us as men to grow our families, spiritually that is, through leadership and an understanding of the will of God. We have been blessed with God-given abilities and responsibilities to our families. Who will lead them if we don't? When I look around in the community and see single mothers trying to raise growing boys, grandparents having to deal with teenagers, aunts and uncles single-handedly dealing with another man's children, I see a lack of discipline, love and understanding of God's will from the original fathers. As an aggregate population we are failing our children. Men must step up and become leaders, and it all starts with a man's family. Some instances are unavoidable, but for the most part, these families are struggling from a lack of leadership because a father has failed to realize his role as a man. These days being a father, a good father, is considered an option rather than a requirement once the baby comes, and this must soon change.

Now the concept of male leadership and the ability to lead a family is applied twofold to pastors. They have two families to lead – the one at home and the one at church. While both are intertwined and often involved in helping grow and develop the other, they are inherently separate organisms. And that's what a family is: an organism. It must be fed, it must rest, it must work and it must grow. It is a living, vibrant organism, and the moment it becomes stagnant, the family fails to thrive. As men we are called to feed the family, to lead it to the love of God.

I've often asked if a pastor can't control his own children, that is, if he fails as a leader at home, how can he be entrusted with the responsibility of leading God's flock? As a pastor, I am the central leader and example by which the rest of the church operates. Christ is our supreme example, and all men and women are called to live as Christ did, but in our world the pastor is the standard bearer, and fair or not, he is held accountable as such. How often do we read news stories about men cheating on their wives or getting caught doing drugs? Not terribly often because such occurrences are considered common in this day and age. But if a pastor is caught cheating on his wife or doing drugs, the story hits the front page the next day. It's the lead story for the local news; it is editorialized and scrutinized to a degree few others experience. Whether or not our culture is willing to admit it, society looks to pastors to set a spiritual standard, and it is our duty to uphold that standard to the greatest degree possible.

Much of what is wrong in the world today starts within the home. I set out from the beginning to make certain my children never cursed at police officers, disrespected teachers or bad-mouthed adults. My family would be one of respect and composure. There is a great deal of planning that goes into starting a family, just as there is a great deal of planning that goes into starting a church. Before I ever had a child, I began pondering how I would lead my family. Preparation, prayer and thought are essential when beginning any journey, great or small.

Likewise, I began wondering how to ensure the members of our congregation were raising their children correctly. So Gloria and I started teaching Bible classes on Wednesday nights and soon transitioned those classes into marriage classes. We had plenty of problems during our first few years of marriage, so we were pleased to help the couples at our church. We wanted them to learn from our mistakes.

Lorea's birth marked an important chapter in the growth of my family because she was the fruit of our prayers and patience. Our years of trials and waiting had been rewarded with a child. God was telling Gloria and me that He was working in His time and we were welcome to trust that He knew best. With that trust in mind we set out to grow our church family. I had faith that the Holy Spirit would show me how to lead His people, just as He would show me how to lead my family at home.

Gloria has never caused me any embarrassment, which is both a testament to her relationship with God and a compliment to me as the leader of our family. God blessed me with both a wife and children who honor the Lord and with the ability to lead them.

Now at this time I was still working as an insurance salesman. I was pastoring a church and leading a group of insurance agents when the company decided to discontinue the insurance product we had been selling. The company sent me home sickened by the loss of my insurance agency and the financial impact this would have on my agents and me. Suddenly, I was broke. My company filed bankruptcy which meant I had to get out of the business. I was hired by another company, but the pay wasn't enough so I went to another job, then another and finally landed in unemployment.

I was left with a couple of new families – Gloria and Lorea and a burgeoning church. Broken and relying on faith and trust, I went to God and He told me I was only meant to pastor His church. He told me to focus on Him, lead His people and He would take care of my family and me. What else could I do? With that I became a full-time pastor and left behind my quest for another full-time job to focus on building the church physically and spiritually.

The church growth exploded, but at home we were still enduring hard times. God's plan was working out in our little community, but the church contributions were not adequate enough to support the church and me. The financial struggles continued and I decided I knew my home situation better than God. He would soon remind me that He was in charge. I found a part-time job fixing up old cars and selling them for a little profit, and Gloria went back to work as a school teacher. Soon I was cut off from selling cars because the state of Georgia legislated the need for a license to sell more than three cars per year. Again, I was back to being a full-time minister. I had tried to be a minister and a full-time worker, then a minister and a part-time worker, but God's plan was going to be accomplished through me in spite of me. My side jobs were finally put to rest, and God's job was brought to the forefront.

The pastor is a parallel with Christ because he is the head of his local church and shepherds the flock in the same way Jesus is the head of the body of believers and shepherds us. That responsibility comes with a level of personal leadership that requires a pastor to make autonomous decisions. A church must bestow a certain amount of trust upon a pastor because it cannot be a truly democratic organism. Mass chaos would break out if every decision in the church had to be voted on by every member of the congregation. Little would get done and churches would experience great division. Few things dissolve relationships and split people more than openly democratic voting. Look at our nation during every presidential voting year. Families and friends are divided by a single vote and the ramifications last for months, sometimes years. To that end, a pastor needs to make decisions about church business, often with the help of his board, without the prior approval of the congregation. I've had members come up to me and tell me that God has said to them that if the whole congregation runs around the building, we will raise the money for a new sanctuary. I usually tell them that if God lets me know, we will do it, but until then, we'll go about fundraising the normal way – sacrificially. Everyone wants to have a revelation and stand out front leading the people, but this is why the congregation must rely on and trust its pastor. For the sake of God's orderly world and the well-being of the church, congregations must trust that a pastor is doing God's will, praying and constantly reading God's Word.

We sought to make our worship services exciting. People should come to church and be inspired, otherwise they might as well stay home. Additionally, we wanted to see our members return home and apply the teachings of the Bible to their lives away from the church. It's easy to come to church and get excited about the music and receive a powerful message, but everyday life should reflect those biblical teachings. When we are surrounded by people of God, in a place of God, worshipping God, it's not difficult to give testimony of what God is doing in our lives. But it gets harder to maintain an attitude of worship at home, at work, at the store or in our neighborhoods. I'm thankful that people get excited in church, are inspired by the services and have a good time worshipping God, but if they leave that spirit at church, something is wrong. That's why I have always done my best to explain the Bible as simply as possible with hope it will motivate the congregation to study the Bible more in English and in the original Hebrew and Greek. The deeper God's children delve into His Word, the better they will be equipped to listen when He talks and rely on His promises when faced with adversity.

People have always enjoyed our worship style because they feel free to worship the Lord in their own way. We like to get excited by singing and shouting. It's fun to get excited about worshipping God, and it's biblical to be excited about worship. On the other hand, we don't believe in the unknown tongues because the tongues at Pentecost were understood through interpretation. Some people like to say that they speak in tongues so Satan doesn't know what they're saying, but for Satan to be Satan he needs to know every language, so I don't buy that reason. For those reasons we don't trust anyone utilizing tongues without interpretation. If someone were to stand up in our church and start speaking in an unknown tongue without interpretation, we would call him or her out in the name of the Lord because we have always been a church of biblical doctrine. Fortunately we have never had that problem during my 25-plus years as a pastor.

Now we also tried to stay away from Sunday night services. Some pastors don't like to see the church close down on a Sunday night; they think the church should be open all day on Sunday. I would rather see families spend time together on Sunday afternoons, so we've always had our church services in the morning. I like to say that I keep them twice as long in the morning so they don't have to come back in the evening. I believe it is important for our members to spend quality time together with their families on Sunday evening. So unless I have a special guest coming for a specific event on a Sunday evening, I don't hold evening services.

Gloria and I poured our hearts into the church. After several years, we witnessed it grow from the 35 to 50 member congregation we had when we first started the church to around 500 members. Life was good and the hard times were starting to fade away. God was building my two families and promised me continued growth. He was blessing me with security and enabling me to grow as a pastor and leader of men and women. I was coasting through pastoring and in the process I became more involved in church activities. We had programs and events at the church constantly, and I made sure I was there for all of them so the people could get to know and love their pastor. It was important to me that I was a face at the church for activities, not just someone who stands in the pulpit to preach at people. Unfortunately, in all my zealous focus I started to neglect a very important aspect of my life, something more important than any church event – my family at home.

3
_____

THE EPIPHANY

Being a pastor is not an easy job. Many congregants see a pastor for a few hours each week and consider little else in terms of his work week. But working at a church is much like working on a movie set or a television show. Dozens, maybe hundreds, of people are involved in planning and practicing for worship services throughout the week. Days of preparation go into a service that lasts just a few hours. Similarly, several months of time and effort are put into producing a two hour movie. In both cases, the congregations/audiences see only a fraction of the work that goes into the final product. They only see a finished, polished presentation.

Of course, for a pastor, the objective is not to entertain, but to inspire God's people through teaching and preaching the Word of God.

I don't say this so my congregation will feel sorry for me, or to apologize for any pastor who has ever seemed too tired to strike up an enthralling conversation at a moment's notice. No, I say this to warn pastors and future pastors about the dangers of mixing up priorities and to encourage all of us to take a look at how we treat our two families.

Fellowship Bible Baptist Church continued to grow and prosper after the early years of blessing and struggle. By 1987 our church had grown to around 500 members, and we were enjoying fruitful worship in our sanctuary, stretched beyond our building's capacity each Sunday. After much prayer and consideration we decided to expand our facilities by building a new sanctuary that would triple our capacity. We had plans made and received bids from various contractors, but they all seemed too high, beyond what we were willing and able to spend. As the leader, I had a lot of decisions to make. Ultimately, I became the church's general contractor to save money.

My family at home continued to grow and prosper as well. Gloria and I were blessed with the birth of our first son El, and he and Lorea were the joys of our lives. We tried to impress the importance of God to our children while also balancing our time between them. The growth of the church mirrored the growth of my family, and the two were stretching me to my limit.

This process isn't new to any man, though. While pastors are certainly stretched and pressured to spend a great deal of time at church, all jobs create priorities and stress for fathers and mothers. Business professionals, doctors, teachers, mechanics. No one is immune from the pressures of work and how they impact the ability to lead and love a family, especially in today's fast-paced world. We have become more industrialized, expected to work like machines and to leave all our troubles at home.

I wasn't unlike these other men and women. Growing up, my father was often absent from our everyday lives. I felt he spent too much time and effort developing his church than in shepherding our family. However, I have come to appreciate that he was doing what he believed was God's will. A preacher's son has one great advantage over any deacon, elder or associate pastor in a church – he sees a pastor at home. A daughter becomes more like the eyes of God in a pastor's life because she sees exactly what a pastor does and cares little about his motive. A son only wants to spend time with his father, to develop an intimate relationship and to pour his love into his father, just like the Lord. We could learn a lot from the words and experiences of children because they are not affected by the world's influence. More than money, toys, clothes or nice houses, our children just want us.

I learned this painful, difficult, and ultimately valuable lesson from El one day at my office. At the age of five, El was visiting me at the church on an otherwise normally busy day. The church was growing steadily and I was constantly pressured with more responsibility. Life was good, but busy.

In those days I kept a large calendar on my desk to ensure an organized schedule. Every day was planned out, and the calendar was consistently filled up weeks in advance. El was playing in my office one day, and while I stepped out of the room, he climbed onto my desk and began looking through my calendar. As he looked across the weeks on the calendar, each day was filled. El searched through the month printed on that first page, and finding no openings, he turned the page to the next month. He found a clear date several weeks in the future and wrote the most poignant message I've ever received in my life. When I returned to the office and sat down in my chair to look at what he had been up to, I found El's scribbled note written on the calendar. "Spend time with El." Here was my five-year-old son attempting to schedule time with his dad by making an appointment. I'll never forget what I saw on my calendar that day.

Tears welled in my eyes as I put everything away. I immediately took the rest of the day off and went home to play with my son. I felt ashamed, sad and foolish for relying on my five-year-old son to point out a sin in my life. My priorities were based around my work at the church instead of my family. We played together that afternoon and I knew my life had changed that day. It had to. I immediately revisited all the memories of my childhood, growing up wanting my father to be there for me and play with me. I didn't want my kids to grow up wishing the same things.

In my flashback I began to consider my father's example as a dad and husband. I learned from what he taught me and how he raised me, and I wanted to make sure I had learned from his standard, understanding he had great moments and poor moments as a father.

My dad worked hard in his quest to feed and clothe his wife and eight children, but it often seemed we came second to the church. We lived in the city of Eatonton, GA, but the three churches my father pastored were 64 miles away. Every Sunday morning we would wake up early and have to drive to one of the three churches, spend the day at the church and arrive home late Sunday evening.

It's not always easy growing up a pastor's child. We had enough to get by, but as a child I felt that the God of Abraham, Isaac and Jacob didn't bring us much in the way of clothes, food and shelter. Every Christmas I would pray and ask God to send me some new clothes, a bike or something to play with, and every Christmas I was disappointed. I often felt like a child without hope, and our lack of income made it difficult for me to trust God as a provider.

The problem wasn't necessarily that we lacked money, but that I didn't understand God's purpose and place as a provider. We had food to eat and a place to stay. God supplied our needs, but I didn't know what that meant. As a father myself, I set out to help my children better understand what God has in store for His people.

My father was a hard man, one who believed in his children stepping up to challenges. I remember my first day of school I got sick and had to come home from school, which was right across the street from our house. When my father came home from his routes – he drove the school bus in the mornings – my mother told him that I was too sick to go to school. While I was truly sick, my father also correctly guessed that I didn't want to go to school. He came back to my room and got me out of bed. Waking me up, my dad told me that I had better get up and go to school. He said I had 12 years to go to school and there was nothing I could do about it because I had to stay for all 12 years. He sent me back to school to find my classroom and I sat there all day. When the bell rang at the end of the day, my teacher looked over as I sat in my seat watching the other students leave. She told me I could go home, but I refused. "My dad says I have to stay here for 12 years before I can come home," I protested. The teacher had to physically take me home, all the while assuring me that I didn't have to stay in the actual school building for 12 years. I don't know that I was ever convinced.

Perseverance was a lesson I wanted to instill in my children. I made sure they learned the importance of hard work and sticking through small setbacks. They also learned quickly that an education was the most important thing they could attain outside of a profound love for the Lord. My father always pushed me and that was what I wanted to do for my children because it would ensure they reached their goals and realized their dreams.

On the other hand, I remember my father often working late, even the night shift, and thus was unable to be home with us in the evening. While we knew about God and the Gospel through church and my father's teaching about the Lord when he was home, my brothers, sisters and I weren't always engaged in the Word of the Lord through consistent bible study and prayer. Though I believe my dad did the best he could in light of the surrounding circumstances, I wanted to make sure I was home with my children at night. I wanted to get home and pray with them and spend time with them, making sure they knew about God from my actions at home rather than my words at church alone. This would further instill a true faith in their lives, or at least an example of true faith.

When I accepted Christ at the age of 14, I did so solely for the purpose of joining the church because I knew this would make my parents happy. And though they were happy, I was not saved. I professed Jesus from my mouth but not from my heart, and in God's eyes that doesn't quite fly. From that moment I lived many years with a mask on, walking around pretending to be saved in Christ.

By the time I graduated high school, I was tired of being under my father's leadership – like most kids that age. In 1969 my parents dropped me off at Fort Valley State College and I said to myself, "I'll miss them, but I'm ready to get on with my life and become a great man." For me, life was about having fun with girls and partying every night. My shallow faith led to my attitude and some poor lifestyle choices during college and afterward.

From my college experiences, I knew I needed to instill in my children the values and qualities that constitute a strong Christian faith. My faith had been based on my father's job as a pastor and the approval of my parents when it should have been grounded in a foundation of the knowledge of God. I sought to teach my children what the saving grace of Christ is all about.

I may have had good intentions, but my fervor for being at church was misguided at best. I truly believe that if everyone abided by the laws of God with regard to the family, we would change the world. There would be no sexually transmitted diseases, there would rarely be any broken homes and poverty would be greatly reduced because two parents would be supporting each family. The reason God gave us laws and examples to live by is because He knows the best way for us to worship Him and live, and He wants us to be strong and live well. Until El's message, I hadn't been abiding in God's will as a husband and father, but I was determined to make a drastic change in my life – one that would honor my wife, my children and most importantly, God.

4

THE CHANGE

El's note changed my life. With that one phrase my world was turned upside down, and I learned the importance of a pastor's priorities. A lifetime as a pastor's son, years of being a pastor myself, attendance at elder's meetings and conventions, nothing got through to me until my 5-year-old son climbed onto my desk and wrote the kind of wisdom that could only come straight from God. I shouldn't have had to rely on my young son to reveal my faults, but I'm glad he did it. This just goes to show that God can use anyone to convey a message.

Lorea, El and Ryan would experience a new kind of father for the rest of their lives, and Gloria would always know she was my queen. They became my number one priority on this earth. My family understood that God would always come first, but from that day forward, they would know without a doubt that I was in the business of being a father before anything else.

Through El's words I realized I could not be a super pastor, someone who took the weight of the world, or at least the entire congregation, on his shoulders. I had been so accustomed to handling everything myself, being at the church from dusk until dawn and leading my church family to the point of exhaustion. I didn't want to delegate, more importantly I didn't know if I could trust others with what I considered my work. I quickly learned from this experience that I had been considering the church my responsibility and my child, as opposed to God's responsibility. I thought the church lived and breathed because I willed it, and only I could see to it that everything was done correctly for God. This was not what God wanted, and it isn't what He wants from any father or husband.

How can we as pastors expect our congregations to follow us on Sundays if we don't practice what we preach the other six days of the week? A pastor who cannot lead his family at home has little business leading his church family. He has no basis for teaching others. Of course no one is perfect all the time. Pastors – just like other people – foul up from time to time. But as the leader of a body of believers, a pastor faces a certain scrutiny that requires he step up and live as closely to Christ as possible. This is for the sake of his family, the church and the reputation of the Gospel to the world. The pastor's family is unique with regard to this concept because it sees the real version, the authentic man at home. His attitude, his habits and his feelings are all stretched to their limits at home, and his handling of that pressure is the ultimate representative of his ability to lead a larger group of God's children. I am thankful I realized my duty to my family, so that I could pastor my church without an air of hypocrisy. My family conveyed to my congregation that I could be trusted as a leader because I led them at home just as I led my family at church. I strove to be the same kind of man in both places at all times.

The same is true for men outside the church. We are all called first to lead our families. Strong fathers and husbands do more for their families than they could ever do as strong businessmen. Being a strong, hard-working man on the job is important to a family's survival, but it's more important to be a strong, hard-working man at home.

Unfortunately, pastors seem to get a free pass to neglect their families. Congregants, elders, other pastors, even the family at home think, "He's doing God's work, so how can I criticize him for spending too much time at the church?" It seems contrary to rebuke a pastor for doing too much at church since he has a responsibility to lead. God's work is more important than anything else isn't it? And isn't it most important to spread the Gospel of Christ – a pastor's primary contribution to his community? All of these statements are true, but they all must begin in the home. A pastor is first a father and husband who should embrace these roles under guidance from God. His family at home should be enveloped in the Gospel, feel loved and appreciated and truly know the relationship between Christ and the church.

Pastors should be open to constructive criticism because they are God's vocational spiritual leaders. However, some pastors get away with sin for far too long because people are afraid to confront them. This trend must stop in our churches and in the homes of spiritual leaders because everything launches from the home. Life falls into the right place as long as we trust in the Lord and ask for His guidance in doing His will.

With a new understanding of my priorities and a commitment to change, I set about delegating responsibility. My family became more important to me than the need to make certain I was attending every church function. One of the hardest aspects of this new life was that I had to learn to trust others with tasks I'd spent my life accomplishing. How does a pastor turn "his" church over to others? He learns to appreciate the fact that all this work is God's work. Once I was able to pass credit to the Lord, I realized how much easier it was to delegate responsibility. I became proud of what my associate pastors, elders, deacons and volunteers were accomplishing. This gave me a new perspective on God's impact in the life of His followers. All those years I'd been burning my candle at both ends, while people had been waiting on the sidelines, longing to help and contribute to God's work in and around Fellowship Bible Baptist Church.

I talked with my children at night to make sure I understood what was going on in their lives. I didn't want them to have questions that went unanswered, and if I didn't have the answer, I wanted to assure them I would soon get one. It became more important for me to make sure my children had lunch money for the next day at school than it was for me to be at every prayer meeting at the church. I devoted myself first to God and then to my family. Gloria and I encouraged our children to develop their God-given skills and abilities for the purpose of honoring

God in their lives. El told me at a very young age that he wanted to play professional football, so we sat him down and told him about the perseverance and focus it was going to take to accomplish that goal. We started playing with him in the backyard, running drills and throwing and catching the football. I taught him how to take a hit because no one can play football if he is scared of a little pain. I showed El how to hit the dirt and go after the ball. We observed other children leaving the field after football practice wearing uniforms that weren't the least bit dirty. Football is dirty sport, not ethically but physically. Boys playing football are expected to get down in the mud when going after the ball. We told El that we weren't training a soft football player because it is an oxymoron. The same philosophy went for Ryan when he decided to play football too. We refused to have soft, weak sons playing a contact sport. Both of our boys showed they were tough, which was positive because that's what football requires; it would be wrong to teach them otherwise. Too many parents are fearful that their child will be fatally injured every time he takes a hit in a contact sport like football. These parents should not allow their children to participate in this kind of sport if they feel this way. We were never reckless with El's health for we always ensured he wore protective gear and made certain he was as safe as possible. One of the best things Gloria and I did for El's and Ryan's football careers was to allow them to play without our getting in the coaches' business and without overreacting after every hit they took. We recognized that when parents get too deeply involved in the coaches' job, the children suffer.

In addition, we taught our children to be respectful of teachers and coaches because they are virtually one in the same. The most important quality for an athlete to have is to be coachable. One may have exceptional ability, but if he or she isn't coachable, athletic prowess doesn't do any good. I went as far as to tell my kids that if a coach curses them out or gets in their face, they were to sit there and take it because without determination and discipline, an athlete cannot effectively compete on the field or in this world. The reason so many people start their children in athletics at a young age is because sports teach children the values and qualities they will need to succeed in the real world. Coaches are teachers of these qualities and values.

Today too many children have the attitude that they don't have to do everything they are told by their parents or other authority figures. They are quick to say, "This is a free country, and I've got my rights." We all have rights and privileges to an extent, but few parents are teaching their children what it means to learn and persevere. We are raising a generation of intelligent quitters. Education has never been at such a high and advanced level, but in cramming our children's heads full of all this knowledge, many parents have failed to teach them how to persist during hard times.

After a successful high school football career, El received a full scholarship to play football at his first choice, Florida State University. During his college years, El was voted Most Valuable Player of the 2006 FedEx Orange Bowl against Penn State University. God rewarded El's hard work, endurance and persistence to accomplish his goal of being drafted into the National Football League where he currently plays wide receiver for the Pittsburgh Steelers. More importantly, we had taught him that he could honor God through his football career and today he is a God-fearing man who makes his family proud every day.

Ryan, an incredible athlete in his own right, also wanted to play football as well as basketball and baseball. We relied on the knowledge we gained from El's experiences playing sports to motivate Ryan as well. Gloria and I also challenged Ryan to be the best football player he could be, and he now attends college on a full football scholarship, realizing his dream and doing so for the purpose of honoring God.

Lorea was a multiple-sport player engaged in track and field as well as basketball until she injured her foot in high school and was forced to quit everything but swimming. Even then, we installed a swimming pool at home so she could practice and enjoy swimming. Nothing was too much when it came to supporting our children in their endeavors, both academically and athletically. After college, Lorea began working at the church with me as our ministry coordinator. I am so thankful to God for the privilege of working side-by-side with my wife and daughter in the church. It's wonderful to see my family's intense involvement in the church. I could never have been engaged in my children's lives with such impact had I been spending all my time at the church. I would have missed out on the countless hours of fun with them and priceless memories from the backyard to various sporting arenas.

Gloria is a vibrant, active, friendly and committed first lady because she loves the Lord. She stands firm in the God's Word and doesn't cause shame to me or the membership. She recognizes her place as a woman, wife and mother by showing her appreciation of me as her husband and pastor. It's important for a pastor's wife to be an upstanding woman and person. If people attend a church with an unfriendly, gossiping, bossy, ignorant pastor's wife, they are often turned off to the entire church. It doesn't matter what the pastor says or what the membership does, it only takes one unpleasant experience like a sour look on her face to turn a person or a family off from church completely. For the last 30-plus years, Gloria has been the backbone of this ministry in that she is my critic, consultant, confidant and best friend. When she said her marriage vows and promised to stick with me through everything, she meant what she said.

El's simple note changed more than my priorities, it helped me realize the need to trust God with my work. I had been trying to play a role that one man wasn't meant to play. The only man meant to lead all churches, to attend all functions, to take on the responsibility of saving the world is Jesus Christ.

5

THE MENTORS

God doesn't want to see us fail. He enjoys seeing His children succeed in His name and prosper for the betterment of His kingdom. Unfortunately, since the beginning of time, we have been spectacular failures. This is why I find it is incredibly important to have mentors. How can you know what to do without having been there before? Learning through experience is what the majority of us do in so many aspects of life, and while that may work, there is a better way to succeed. Mentors are vital to growth because they've been there and done that. You have their history to learn from so you don't have to make the same mistakes. It is also important to note that I didn't necessarily stay with the same mentor throughout my life. During different stages of ministry and the evolution of a church, a pastor requires different mentors and leaders. There was nothing insulting about moving on to a new mentor because I needed something different from a new and fresh leader.

When I started growing a church, I sought out mentors who could teach, guide and show me how to grow this family into a body of believers longing to honor the Lord. It is much easier to travel with a guide, after all. My father was my first mentor in that he taught me to first seek God's direction in everything. Mentors help you get where you want to go because they've already been there before. So when I set out in ministry I looked at my church and other churches. I spoke with Pastors Harold Rawls and Walter Glover and asked them how to get to where they were since their churches had about 500 members each and mine had only 30 members.

Pastor Rawls and Pastor Walter Glover, head of the local Baptist Association, led ministries for years and had grown them to successful, sizable numbers. Most importantly, they were impacting their respective communities for God and I wanted to do that too. Pastor Rawls had ordained me and licensed me to become a preacher. I sought his guidance because he was the one to see the quality of a shepherd in me, believing I was one who could lead a congregation. Pastor Glover was a man who led well and was an incredible preacher with strong followers. In those early years I looked to these men a great deal because I was starting out with just a mustard seed of faith and a supportive wife. While that's more than some preachers start with, I knew I needed the support of mentors to be successful at the level I thought I should reach.

Once my church had grown to a similar size, around 500 people, I sought out new mentors to help me learn how to grow a church to around 1,000 people. In 1985 while attending a workshop given by Pastor Jasper Williams of Salem Baptist Church in

Atlanta, GA, I was struck by his style and the success of his church. He offered me new motivations and taught me many exciting things to help reach more people in my community.

Once Fellowship Bible Baptist had grown larger than 1,000 people, I began utilizing Pastor Rick Warren as my mentor. With a congregation of over 22,000 people, who better to look to than the man pastoring one of the largest churches in America? In addition to pastoring Saddleback Community Church, Pastor Warren is the well known author of the "Purpose Driven Life" series, and has been a man with a vision of reaching millions around the world. After meeting Pastor Warren I learned how he grew his church, increased contributions and did the work of God to impact his community to the nth degree. Pastor Warren was one of the men who helped motivate me to look toward the future of Fellowship Bible Baptist Church and see the vision of a new community center and the Dome, our larger worship center.

Mentors can teach you from their experiences, but it shouldn't stop there. Many pastors publish books to offer wisdom and guidance to readers and pastors alike. I often read books by pastors who have much to teach me about different aspects of ministry that I don't necessarily get from my mentors. One of the most important things a pastor can do is to maintain a broad perspective and always be on the look out for resources that can help better or improve his ministry for God.

I can't write about mentors without including my biblical mentors, men I emulate and who have helped me develop my creed to save the lost at any cost. The Apostle Paul may not be a mentor to me in the traditional sense – though he did a pretty good job with St. Timothy – he is as important to my mission as any other man in my life. Paul had a soul-winning heart. He was willing to lay down his life for the sake of the Gospel. Beyond that, Paul was willing to be separated from God so that the lost could know the Lord and be saved. He was also willing to go to Hell, to experience eternal separation from God. This was all for those who spat on him, put him in prison and didn't know the loving salvation of Jesus.

He is truly a man to admire and revere. Few people have influenced the world to the degree of Paul. Even with all my love for saving others, I wouldn't be willing to go to Hell for someone else. I might die for them, but to go to Hell for people you don't know, let alone for someone you love, is beyond my realm of reasoning.

My mentors have been people who've been down a road I am interested in exploring. While they always take a backseat to the power of God's Word in my life, I know I wouldn't be where I am today without the profound influence of my mentors.

6

THE HOUSE

A church is not made of wood, bricks, concrete and a steeple. Those are the materials of the church building. A home is not made of solid materials, but of people. Likewise, churches consist of a body of Christ followers, residing in close-knit communities, who build their faith on a foundation of love, trust, tradition and a belief in the redeeming grace of Jesus Christ.

Communities enjoy meeting in church buildings in the same way families enjoy living in homes. To accommodate the masses that were pouring in each Sunday, we decided to build a new sanctuary. I have always been a proponent of debt-free construction, and I didn't want the church's ability to thrive and survive to be limited by debt and the struggles of managing debt. The congregation was behind the plan. From the beginning we set out to raise the money for the new sanctuary and trust that God would deliver our land and buildings.

As we gradually bought and paid for the land on Dunbar Road, we slowly built the structures. I'm thankful we had the foresight to purchase 10 acres of land at that time because this enabled us to keep the church in the same area and continue impacting the same community. Sometimes I look back and reflect on the plans we made to house the number of parishioners we would eventually experience. It seems silly now to build a sanctuary for a certain sized congregation because you never know how many people we will have. Why build for 300 and soon have 1,000? It seems we should have just built for 1,000 from the start, but it is easy to say that from this position in time.

We started the first building program one Sunday when I stood before the congregation and held up twenty dollars and said, "Here is $20. We're going to start with the first block. Blocks cost 50 cents each. I don't know how many blocks $20 will buy, but I'm ready to get started." At the end of the day we had about $600, and we began building the church the next week. We paid for and constructed the church block-by-block, asking people only how many blocks they could donate.

We eventually completed the exterior walls and needed to put the roof on, but we couldn't afford the trusses that support the roof. Then a member of our church came to me one Sunday and said he'd just gotten a bonus at work. He would pay for the roof. So he gave $1400 that day, and we were able to complete our new church building.

The congregation grew to around 500 members within five years, with a regular attendance of 350 on Sunday mornings. Our church capacity was only 275, so we knew it was time to build again. Once again, we wanted to build the new sanctuary on a cash-only basis. Just as before, I wasn't interested in putting our church in debt for the sake of building a new structure. We started the building fund and began shopping the project to different contractors in and around Warner Robins. I also made certain the church board maintained autonomous control over the building. The church members had to understand that the church was not an investment they owned. When people sign their names to something, they think they have certain rights and control, but that wasn't what our church was going to be about. This was God's church.

After four and a half years of fundraising, we received bids on the project with the lowest bid being $860,000. Both the board and I believed we could do the project for less if we built it ourselves. At that time I became the general contractor on the project and sub-contracted out the construction. Once again we started building the new sanctuary piece-by-piece. I would oversee the building site, and when we needed building materials or wanted to add something to the building, I would go to the board and have them review and approve expense reports.

It wasn't always easy. Building contractors would often come by the site and offer to put several hundred thousand dollars in our account and take over the project. When working out in the hot sun, doing things on your own and with as many volunteers as you can muster, that gets tempting. We were erecting a building, broke and trying to do it debt-free, and it would have been easy to let the professionals come in and do the job. Instead we trusted God to supply our needs in building His church. I felt that God would cut me off at the path if I gave in, so I promised to do it honestly, straight, fair and right. God told us to be careful with how we build His kingdom. On October 11, 1992 we turned the key and opened the doors to our completed 1,000-seat sanctuary and office building having spent just $525,000.

That was one of the greatest days in the life of our church. We were so proud that we'd come together as a community and constructed this church with our own money, sweat and hard work. When we first opened the building in 1992, about 500 people were in attendance, and the sanctuary was only half full. I remember wondering what it would take to fill up the pews, but God honored His promise to us because we had built the church according to His plans and His will. He brought new people into our community and helped us reach out to thousands more. But it didn't take long for us to push the walls of that church building too. By 1995 we had grown to about 2,000 members and began having two services every Sunday.

The church and I quickly realized we needed more space if we were going to relevantly reach the community for Christ. We had plans drawn up for another worship center to be built debt-free. It was our philosophy that if the church's money wasn't going toward a mortgage, we could better serve the congregation and the community and provide job opportunities for the unemployed. I don't believe in begging for money. People come to church to hear the Gospel preached because they are longing for Jesus Christ, who is the only one to quench their thirst for the spirit. We are here to serve and show them the way to the Lord. Money turns people off, so through our services, events and television ministry, we always made a point not to talk about money. That way, people could feel the conviction of the Holy Spirit and let God lead them in giving money. So many people think preachers are all about money. When visitors accepted Jesus Christ as Lord and Savior, we saw to it that they were taught the principles and purposes of giving, but first and foremost, we wanted visitors and the surrounding community to know that our church was about spreading the Gospel of Christ.

We saved more money and managed to build a Fellowship Community Center to give local kids a wholesome place to go after school. Instead of hanging out on street corners, in fast food places and other problem areas, kids in our community would have a safe place to hang out. Here they could play basketball or other indoor sports, do their homework and wait for their parents to pick them up. These days too many children would rather go to the arcade and play video games or surf the Internet. But we were hopeful folks in the church, and especially those outside the church, would be more interested in coming to the Community Center for fellowship and fun. In addition, we built a large barbeque pit and cleared a field for outdoor events. All of this was done in order to better serve the Warner Robins community and welcome it with the love that God had shown us.

We've had several ministries at Fellowship Bible Baptist Church that were not successful from a financial perspective or the feasibility of continuance. We once operated a Christian school for kindergarten through fifth-grade, but had to shut it down. Our church also operated a book store that had to be closed. Fortunately, when you are working for the Lord, success is measured in faithfulness, not in monetary gain or fame. The best we can ever do is to attempt to follow the Lord and listen when He talks to us, which is what I've always tried to do in building and leading this church.

Once again life was good. We bought an additional 40 acres of land across the street from the Fellowship campus, bringing the church's property total up to 50 acres. The congregation continued growing. Gloria and I were reaping some of the financial blessings of God's bounty. We were comfortable for the first time since I lost the insurance agency. But this was God's queue to check us in our faith. It is easy to be faithful when rewards happen quickly and blessings abound, but God truly reveals our hearts in the face of trials. Six months after we purchased the land across the street from the church, I was diagnosed with diabetes.

7

THE TRANSPLANT

God isn't interested in His people living comfortable, cushy lives on earth; He is interested in sharpening us to make us better for Him. He builds us up by first breaking us down, for God is interested in our giving glory to Him.

Throughout my life I've faced challenges, and since becoming a follower of Christ I've always come out on the other side with a better understanding of who God is and who He wants me to be. From losing our house due to bankruptcy in 1982, to the early struggles of guiding a family at home and at church,

God has placed several obstacles in my life to sharpen me to His will. And it has worked. One scary thing about getting comfortable and experiencing abundant blessing is that God is working His plan on His schedule, not ours. Extreme levels of comfort sometimes precede extreme levels of challenge.

My great trial started in 1998 with a diagnosis. I was once an overweight man, but having diabetes broke down my body, which made me start thinking about my overall health. I recognized the human body as a precious thing. I only wish I had the foresight long ago to take better care of myself. But again, it's easy to look back and realize what I had done to myself. What's most important is taking that experience and knowledge and applying it to life in the present – learning from the past to make the future better.

After being diagnosed with diabetes, I made quick changes to my lifestyle, but four months later I woke up with yellow eyes. I went to the doctor and was told I had liver problems. They gave me medicine to clear up my pupils, but my liver was severely

damaged and soon I was going to need a liver transplant. I asked the doctor if they could just do some
kind of bypass to make my liver work, but unfortunately it couldn't be done. I will always remember
staring at the doctor's lips when he said, "There is
nothing else I can do for you." Those are terrifying
words, words nobody ever wants to hear. Those
words knocked me off my feet. The doctor offered to
send me to a specialist at Emory Hospital in Atlanta,
GA to see if anything could be done outside of a
liver transplant, but I couldn't get an appointment
for two months. When you're walking up to Death's
door, two months is too long.

A friend of mine recommended I go to the
Mayo Clinic in Jacksonville, FL because the best spe-
cialists were there, and I could be seen much sooner.
Within days I had an appointment. Gloria and I went
down to see doctors who affirmed that I needed a
liver transplant. They offered me hope, saying they
could fix it, and I would be as good as new if they
could get me a matching liver. They told me I had
three and a half years left on my existing liver, but for

now they could affix a stint inside my liver to drain into a colostomy bag. I wore the bag on my leg for three and a half years. While preaching and pastoring, driving, attending football games and going about day-to-day activities, I always wore that bag on my leg.

I was placed on the liver transplant list at the Mayo Clinic, which was shorter than the one at Emory Hospital. However, Mayo Clinic in Jacksonville, FL was not recognized by my health insurance, so I couldn't have the surgery there. The insurance company referred me back to Emory Hospital for the surgery where I met Dr. Thomas Hefron. He evaluated my case and agreed that I needed to have the liver transplant.

Now as my body was breaking down, the church was growing. Membership was up to 2,800, and God was showing me that the church existed outside of me and my full health. My impaired health turned out to be a blessing because our church was faithful and obedient during my ordeal. The deacons and elders led well and our interim pastor simply kept preaching the Gospel, which is what should happen while the senior pastor is gone. During the time I was out sick and unable to preach, the members stepped up and took ownership of the ministries. Everything at the church went smoothly, which was one less thing for me to worry about. Initially, I was anxious that a church population of this size might leave because I wasn't there preaching every Sunday morning. I realized that if this happens at a church, the pastor hasn't done a good job of preaching the Gospel and teaching the Bible; the congregants would be following the pastor rather than following God. So I was relieved that our church huddled together and kept the faith in the midst of the storm that was my illness. Attendance and offerings remained constant as the church continued on without me, which made me feel good because it meant I had effectively communicated the Gospel to my church family.

During the years of waiting for a donated liver, I experienced many mental changes. Things went through my mind that had never entered it before.

That was when Satan started talking to me. He would show me drunks on the street who cared nothing about their lives, but had good livers. People with healthy body parts were all around me, but they weren't using their bodies for God's kingdom. The devil whispered in my ear, "What do you think about that Willie? Look at all those healthy livers. Those people have never served God in their lives and they get to live and be healthy. Why would your God allow you to suffer like this when you've dedicated your whole life to him?" Satan tried his best to turn me against God, but I realized this was a test. Just like Job, this was my opportunity to show God and all the people around me that I was faithful through my circumstances, both good and bad. God wanted to see if I could back up all that talk because I had preached the love and faithfulness of God to people for two decades. But would I remain faithful when put to the test? I was determined that I would withstand the trial and win for God. Once the Devil saw that I wasn't going to break and I would not abandon my faith, he left me alone for the time being. That's a good feeling – knowing that the Devil gave up on me while God was honored by my faith. Just as God promised, He will never give a Christian anymore than he or she can handle. When we understand that God is with us and will always be with us, we can get through anything. The Devil is destined to lose for he has already lost against Christ. Now it is up to the rest of us to make sure that the Devil keeps losing until his time comes to be cast down into the lake of burning fire. What an honor it is to please God by resisting the Devil. Being a faithful follower was the least I could do.

Every child of God needs to know that everything he or she goes through is a test of faithfulness. God is honored when we praise Him and love Him during the difficult times. So many people love to shout and pray and dance in church, but then they leave, have a little trouble and never come back. We don't take the Devil seriously enough a lot of times. He comes after us with his demons because it's all he has left to do. He wants to see us fail and he wins when a Christian walks out of church and can't handle struggle. It should be an honor to be tempted by the Devil. If the Devil isn't messing with you, you need to look in your life and ask why. Now if he tempts you, you resist and he leaves you alone for a while, that is a victory in Christ. But if the Devil hasn't tempted you in years, or ever, you need to look in your heart and soul and ask yourself if you are living the kind of righteous life that makes the Devil want to take you out. It should truly be an honor that the Devil thinks highly enough of you to give you everything he has. And through all that, God will always stand next to us and show Himself to us if we are willing to look to our side. He is always right beside us, and that was what I had to do during my hard times. When I felt myself start to listen to the Devil, I looked to my side and saw Jesus standing there. He was forever faithful.

The Apostle Paul wrote in his letter to the Philippians, "For to me, to live is Christ and to die is gain." This became my motto during the transplant ordeal because I was ready to live out a longer life for the sake of saving more of the lost, and I was excited about going and being with God. The Apostle Paul had a profound perspective on eternity that he emphasized to the Philippians. When Christians have eternal perspective, they are best prepared to serve the Lord. My options were two of the best options anyone can have – serving the Lord by preaching the Gospel or going to be with the Lord to spend eternity in His presence. If there has ever been a win-win situation, that must have been it.

After three and a half years, I was still waiting for a donated liver. My time was quickly running out. That was when a hero showed himself. Xavier Edwards, my sister Virginia's son, called me to tell me he was going to Emory Hospital to see Dr. Hefron to determine if he would be a match for the transplant. He is my hero because he volunteered to be a living donor by giving me 60 percent of his liver. I asked him if he was sure he wanted to do that for me and he said, "You're my uncle. You've been like a father to me. I look up to you and I want to help save your life." That was a very bold step by a very brave, 31-year-old young man. Lorea had also been tested and was a match as well, but Xavier was a better match and physically better prepared to donate immediately. So Xavier told Lorea not to worry about it anymore, that he was going to take care of me.

On June 5, 2001, Xavier and I went into surgery at Emory Hospital. Xavier went into the operating room and was in surgery for more than eight hours, which seemed like an eternity. Here he was trying to help save my life, but what if he had lost his life on the operating table? I became terrified at the thought, but I was excited to see what God would do with this situation. My family and I were confident that the doctors knew what they were doing as we prayed and put our faith and trust in God, and Xavier came through the surgery fine.

Now it was my turn. I was in surgery for 12 hours as they transplanted Xavier's portion of donated liver into me. Of course Gloria and Virginia were there the entire time. When I came out of surgery I was placed in the Intensive Care Unit. Three days after surgery I developed an intense pain in my back. We talked to the doctors and were told I had developed a blood clot because the portion of Xavier's liver wasn't conforming well enough to my old liver. Imagine, after all that surgery, anxiety and strife, my doctors told me I needed to receive a whole new liver if the transplant was to work. I felt terrible for having put Xavier through all that surgery, but he was proud he had tried to help save his uncle's life. We were assured his liver would grow back completely in 10 days, so Xavier was going to be fine. But now I needed another person's donated liver.

With that transpiring I was deemed in danger and placed at the top of the transplant list. We got one liver, but it had too much fat on it and wouldn't work for me. Then I got a second donated liver from a man who had a motorcycle accident. No one knows how many lives that man's untimely death saved and improved that day, I'm just grateful I got his liver. Because he was an organ donor, his eyes, kidneys, heart and other organs were transplanted to numerous people that night.

The most important thing to me during my suffering was the support of my family. If they had for one moment said, "Well Willie, it was nice know-ing you," I don't think I would have made it through. But because my family had unwavering faith and supported me 110 percent, I was able to come through my transplant stronger because family is what holds people together.

I went back into surgery at Emory Hospital and received the whole liver donated by the unknown donor. I went into the longest, deepest sleep I had experienced in my life.

8

THE NEW LIFE

Four and a half days after the transplant, I opened my eyes and saw Gloria. It was at that point I knew God had brought me through the fire, through the lions' den. My new life began and I haven't looked back since. The transplant changed me more profoundly than almost any other outside occurrence in my life because it made me realize I wasn't made of steel, that I was not invincible. It brought me down to earth. I spent 30 days in the hospital after the liver transplant and an additional two weeks at Emory's rehabilitation house to make certain everything was going well. It was almost two months before I returned to Warner Robins, then two weeks later I resumed preaching. Although I was weak it felt wonderful being back at Fellowship Bible Baptist Church, shepherding my flock.

Thereafter I returned to Emory Hospital weekly to get a check up to evaluate my progress. After some time had passed, they finally took all the tubes out of me. In fact I told Ryan that the first words I wanted to hear when I woke up were, "Dad, the tubes are gone!" I continued to pray that God would heal me and let me live to see Ryan through high school. Since I'd made it through the surgery, I told God I couldn't leave my13-year-old son without his father during high school. Of course since then, I have asked God to let me see him graduate college and see my grandchildren. I'm fortunate God has given me this much time, and I won't complain if He gives me many more years. One thing I know for sure is that I won't take my time on this earth for granted any longer. Life is a vapor.

For a while after the transplant, I felt like a helpless baby. I was completely reliant on medication and my family for my survival. Gloria and Lorea cooked for me and brought me my food; however, some time later I experienced a seizure and had to be continuously watched to make sure I didn't have another attack or get hurt. I wasn't even allowed to drive. Having to rely on others for the most basic life functions and activities humbled me.

Christians should appreciate life more than others because we have the most to live for. We have the light of God in our lives, but too often it takes being in an extreme situation for us to truly appreciate life. My years of trials and tribulations were met with God's blessed healing and elation from my friends and family. Once again, God proved Himself faithful and allowed me to continue leading my two families. I always thought I would be ready to go to God, but this experience taught me that I wanted to delay my departure. To be honest, I was a bit excited about the possibility of seeing Heaven. I love Warner Robins, but when compared to the streets of gold and the crystal seas of Heaven, I think we all know which one a Christian would choose.

But that wasn't God's plan for me. I had more work to do in my church, community and most certainly in my family. While I would have loved to be walking through Heaven with the Lord, I am so thankful for this gift of time with my family. He blessed me with the opportunity to raise Ryan through high school and beyond, to see El realize his dream of playing in the National Football League and to work side-by-side with Lorea at the church.

One of the most incredible things God does with suffering is to bend it to His will so that it will help us better express our love for Him. God strengthened me through my ordeal and in doing so gave me an incredible gift. Yes I was healed of my condition and given the chance to live longer, but more importantly, God gave me a new testimony. Up until this ordeal, my testimony had been about getting saved from my college days of drinking and drugs and living a carefree life. But during my middle-age, God came to me and changed my testimony. He made my liver transplant the most important time in my life by allowing me to show other people that God is the god who heals and saves. Now I can tell people about my struggle as I relate to them on a more profound level.

Another blessing of the transplant and my ordeal is that I gained a new family – all the wonderful people at Emory Hospital who took care of me. We have kept in contact over the years through exchange visits when I go there for checkups and they come down to Warner Robins for my pastor's anniversary and other big events. Everyone always laughs as we share one moment during my hospital confinement. I was so thirsty coming out of my coma that I told one of the nurses I saw an ice cold Miller Lite on a shelf. All I wanted was something to drink, so I practically begged for the Miller Lite. Now they refer to me as the crazy pastor who was under the influence of anesthesia and wanted a beer. Dr. Hefron performed the transplant operation, and we stay close as he continues to advise me on how to keep my liver in good working condition. Without the care of these people I wouldn't be alive today, and for that they have become my life-saving family.

I had to make big changes in my life following the surgery because a donated liver is a delicate thing. Medicine is now a large part of my routine. Basically, it keeps me alive and healthy, but I never thought I would see the day when medicine would be my main routine.

I also had to limit my exposure to dander and pathogens that can lead to infections. My compromised immune system was not going to be my best friend. We started by removing the majority of the carpet in and around my office and home since pathogens flourish in carpet. I quickly became a bit obsessive about keeping away from germs and dirt.

Prior to this I would shake hands with everyone after church services on Sundays, but now I go directly to greet our visitors and then to my office. This transition hasn't been easy because I'm a hugger and a hand-shaker and I love people, but for the sake of my own health I've had to make sacrifices and changes to protect myself in hopes for a longer life to spend with those same friends and family.

The church built a new administrative building, which included a large office for me. It was the members' way of saying thank you for my years of service and for leading the church. As a pastor, it's always nice to have your efforts appreciated, especially when it is aiding in the work of the Lord by impacting lives for Christ. When the church congregants, who have good hearts and souls, show appreciation, I know I must be doing something right.

Furthermore, I limited my workload at the church. After several hours at work in my church office and an hour or so at my personal business, I was exhausted and needed my rest. So I took plenty breaks throughout the day and have since gotten stronger. I can't stay up until 3 a.m. and get up at 6 a.m. any more, but much of my energy is back.

9

EXPANDING ON GOD'S GLORY

Fellowship Bible Baptist Church is also a church-planting community. We are proud to have planted a few churches, including Christian Fellowship Church. It is not only thriving as a church and impacting the military community here in Warner Robins, the pastor has also started a school. This is what the church community should be doing, which is why I refer to it as a community. The purpose of unifying the community under God is to make certain we are able to support one another in Christian love and in all facets of life. A community doesn't survive without multiple levels of support from multiple perspectives and vantage points. Christian Fellowship Church is the grandchild birthed by my former Pastor Rawls who sent me out to start a church almost 30 years ago. It exemplifies why we believe our creed of saving the lost at any cost is so relevant in the community.

We welcomed a Hispanic ministry into our church in 2006 to further reach the community by engaging the Spanish-speaking segment of Warner Robins society. The ministry grew quickly, and prayerfully it will one day occupy our present sanctuary. My vision is to see Fellowship Bible Baptist Church move into its worship center, the Dome, across the street from the current sanctuary and allow the Hispanic ministry to move into our current sanctuary rent-free. The business of doing God's work isn't about making money, regulating people or what we can get for ourselves; it is about helping one another for the sake of God's kingdom. We are all working together for the purpose of spreading God's Word to people around the world. By partnering with this ministry, we are not only impacting the Hispanic community of Warner Robins, we are helping impact the kingdom of God.

Worship in the Dome will offer our congregation the perspective of seeing empty seats again which should remind us of the feeling we had 15 years ago when we walked into our present sanctuary wondering how we would ever fill the 1,000 seats. This event will also remind us that only God can fill 3,000 seats in a single sanctuary.

More is in store for the Dome property site across the street. The master plan is to build senior housing to help take care of our elderly members. In doing so we can be certain their needs are met as well as make it easier for them to access their home church. We also plan to build a food court and recreation center – essentially a multi-use community. Much more has to be done, but I have no other choice but to trust that the Lord will take care of us and believe He will provide the resources and money to build these structures.

When Xavier gave me over half his liver, I promised him I would do something one day to honor him. And even though his liver didn't work out in my body, I wanted to let him know that his willingness to sacrifice was what really mattered. Fortunately, I found an opportunity to raise money for the church building fund and thank Xavier at the same time. I bought vacant land in Warner Robins to develop into a subdivision and named the main street Xavier Edwards Drive. He will always be remembered through this little act of gratitude, and when I sell the property and houses to new families, I will donate the majority of the profits to the Dome. Each of us can help achieve a common goal, and this is my way of leading by example and encouraging the congregation to get the new sanctuary built. When in the midst of fundraising and leading people, the pastor should always be out front setting the standard for the members to follow. That standard should be firmly grounded in the Lord and focused on shepherding a flock.

Looking around to see what else I could do to aid the community, I started a used car dealership, which had once been a part-time adventure, and began selling cars to single mothers and families experiencing hard times. Instead of sending them off to a dealer who would inflate the prices, I would sell them the car at a reduced cost to make sure the families had transportation. This was my little way of trying to further influence the community in a positive manner. Who'd have thought that a little used-car dealership in the low-income community would impact so many lives in a positive way?

We have already entered a new millennium and every day we are a step closer to the return of Christ. From day one, our church creed has been "Save the lost at any cost" and that's what we are going to do. It is my church's mission and my life's mission, and I thank God for every day He gives me to continue living out that creed.

If I've learned anything in my life, it is that family is the most important thing a pastor has other than God himself. When I talk to a young man who wants to pastor a church, I always ask him what his wife thinks about pastoring. I tell him if God has called him to pastor, He has called the family as well. God doesn't keep secrets when it comes to stuff like that. If a wife doesn't want her husband pastoring, I tell him not to pastor. A pastor can't go in a different direction than his family because without the family behind a pastor 200 percent, the pastor has little chance of success. God spoke to Gloria when I began to pastor, and from then on she was passionate about our calling. When your family is with you, there is no mountain you can't move, nothing that can stop you when your work is for the Lord. But if a wife is unwilling or uninterested in being a pastor's wife, the pastor is doomed for failure. Nothing happens unless the family is along side him with burning, passionate support. It is simply the way God intended it.

After my liver transplant, the local newspaper published an article stating that people in my condition are fortunate if they have three years added to their lives. I've never looked at my life in that way because I don't believe you can put a timeline on life. We can't predict what God has in store for us, and we certainly don't know when He plans to take us home to be with Him. It has been seven years since that article was published. Seven years of life to see my children grow into responsible, hard-working, God-fearing adult citizens. Seven years of life to love and honor Gloria as my queen. Seven years for me and I'm still kicking, preaching the Gospel and saving the lost at any cost.

Join Us at:
Fellowship Baptist Church
431 Dunbar Road
Warner Robins, GA 31093
478-929-0828

Service Times
8AM Early Service
9:30Am - Sunday School
10:45AM - Regular Service
Wendesday Bible Study at 7PM
www.fbbchome.org